SELLING SUCCESS:

"MASTERING THE ART OF PERPETUAL SALES"

By

DR FAITH STONES

TABLE OF CONTENTS

Introduction:

In the fast-paced and competitive world of sales, where every interaction is an opportunity and every transaction a milestone, Alex Mason's journey stands as a testament to the transformative power of dedication, resilience, and innovation. As a seasoned sales professional, Alex has weathered the storms of uncertainty and navigated through the peaks and valleys of the market with unwavering determination and a steadfast commitment to excellence. His story is one of triumphs and tribulations, of moments of exhilarating success and challenging setbacks, all woven together by a common thread of relentless pursuit towards long-term success and fulfillment in the dynamic landscape of the sales industry.Through the pages of this novel, we delve into the intricate tapestry of Alex's career, unveiling the secrets and strategies that propelled him from a novice in the world of sales to a revered leader and innovator within his industry. We explore the nuances of customer engagement, the art of effective communication, and the intricacies of building enduring relationships that transcend the boundaries of mere transactions. We unravel the significance of market analysis, risk management, and strategic planning in navigating through economic challenges and market fluctuations, showcasing the resilience and adaptability required to thrive in the ever-evolving sales landscape.Join us on a journey that transcends the confines of traditional sales manuals, as we delve into the heart of what it truly means to sell and keep on selling. Explore the depths of customer psychology, the power of effective storytelling, and the transformative potential of embracing innovation and technology in driving sales excellence. Discover the art of balancing professional commitments with personal well-being, and uncover the transformative power of continuous learning and personal growth in fostering a legacy of enduring success and innovation within the dynamic and competitive realm of the sales industry.Through Alex's story, we invite you to embark on an odyssey of self-discovery and empowerment, where every page unlocks a new insight and every chapter unveils a new dimension of the art of salesmanship. As we delve into the intricacies of Alex's journey, we invite you to reflect on your own experiences and aspirations, and to embrace the transformative potential of dedication, resilience, and innovation in your pursuit of excellence and long-term success in the dynamic and ever-evolving landscape of the sales industry.

Chapters 1:

STRUGGLE IN THE COMPETITIVE SALES INDUSTRY.

I. THE JOURNEY BEGINS

In the bustling metropolis of New York City, where ambition surged through the veins of every resident, a young and determined salesperson named Alex Mason found himself at a crossroads. With a fervent desire to succeed and an unwavering passion for the art of sales, Alex had entered the competitive world of retail with hopes as high as the towering skyscrapers that surrounded him.Raised in a modest neighborhood, Alex had always been driven by the desire to uplift his family's financial situation. His father, a hardworking factory worker, had instilled in him the value of perseverance and the importance of seizing every opportunity that came his way. However, as he navigated the cutthroat world of sales, Alex quickly realized that his earnest enthusiasm alone wouldn't be enough to carve out a place for himself in the fiercely competitive industry.The initial days were a rollercoaster of emotions for Alex. Armed with an unyielding determination to succeed, he embarked on his journey, knocking on countless doors, making phone call after phone call, and attending networking events, all in the pursuit of that elusive first sale. Yet, despite his tireless efforts, rejection became a familiar companion, and the mounting pressure to meet targets began to take its toll on his morale.With each rejection, doubt crept in, threatening to overshadow his once unshakeable confidence. He grappled with self-doubt, questioning his abilities and wondering if he had what it takes to make it in this unforgiving realm of relentless competition. Nights were spent tossing and turning, plagued by the fear of failure and the weight of familial expectations resting heavily on his shoulders.Despite the hardships, there was an indomitable spirit within Alex that refused to yield. Each setback served as a lesson, driving him to analyze his approach and strategize for a different outcome. He immersed himself in books, devoured every piece of sales advice he could find, and sought mentorship from seasoned professionals in the field. Slowly but steadily, he began to comprehend the intricacies of the industry, understanding that success in sales was not just about the gift of the gab but also about resilience, adaptability, and a deep understanding of human psychology.As the chapter drew to a close, Alex stood at the precipice of an uncertain future, determined to turn his struggles into stepping stones toward a brighter tomorrow. With a newfound sense of purpose and a burgeoning arsenal of knowledge, he braced himself for the challenges that lay ahead, ready to carve his own path through the chaotic labyrinth of the sales world.

Chapter 2:

INITIAL SUCCESS AND THE CHALLENGES FACED ALONG THE WAY.

I. THE TASTE OF TRIUMPH AND THE SHADOWS OF ADVERSITY

In the wake of persistent trials and tribulations, Alex Mason's unwavering determination finally bore fruit. After countless rejections and endless perseverance, he secured his first significant sale—a moment that filled his soul with an intoxicating blend of elation and relief. The euphoria of this initial success reverberated through his being, infusing him with a renewed sense of purpose and fueling his aspirations to conquer even greater heights within the cutthroat world of sales.With his first triumph, Alex's confidence soared, and he seized the opportunity to set even higher targets for himself. Armed with a newfound belief in his abilities, he expanded his client base and nurtured stronger relationships with existing customers. His sales figures began to climb, and he found himself being recognized within the organization for his outstanding performance.As his success continued to flourish, however, so did the challenges. Alex soon discovered that the path to sustained triumph was riddled with unforeseen hurdles and fierce competitors who were equally determined to dominate the industry. The taste of initial success served as both a blessing and a curse, amplifying the pressure to consistently surpass previous achievements and maintain an upward trajectory.Amidst the clamor of accolades and the allure of recognition, Alex found himself confronted with the demanding expectations of his superiors and the relentless pursuit of surpassing ever-increasing sales quotas. The demands of the job began to encroach upon his personal life, straining his relationships and leaving him with a gnawing sense of emptiness despite the external validation of his professional accomplishments.Moreover, with his rise in the ranks, Alex encountered resentment and envy from colleagues who perceived his success as a threat to their own ambitions. Office politics reared its ugly head, fostering an environment of mistrust and rivalry that clouded the once vibrant camaraderie he had experienced with his peers. He learned the hard way that success in the cutthroat world of sales often came with the price of navigating through intricate webs of office dynamics and interpersonal relationships.Despite the challenges, Alex remained steadfast in his pursuit of excellence, understanding that every setback was an opportunity for growth and every obstacle a chance to demonstrate resilience. He delved deeper into refining his sales techniques, harnessing his interpersonal skills, and mastering the art of maintaining a delicate balance between ambition and humility.As the chapter drew to a close, Alex grappled with the realization that the journey ahead would demand more than just a strong sales acumen; it would necessitate an unwavering commitment to integrity, a deep understanding of the human psyche, and the resilience to weather the storms of both professional and personal challenges that lay ahead.

Chapter 3:

INTRODUCING THE IMPORTANCE OF UNDERSTANDING CUSTOMER NEEDS AND DESIRES.

I. DECIPHERING THE CODE OF CUSTOMER DESIRES

Amidst the whirlwind of targets, quotas, and intense competition, Alex Mason stumbled upon a pivotal realization that would forever alter his approach to sales: the paramount significance of understanding the intricate tapestry of customer needs and desires. It was a revelation that transcended the superficial transactional nature of sales, leading him to recognize that every successful deal was anchored in a profound understanding of the customer's deepest motivations and aspirations.As he delved deeper into the intricacies of customer psychology, Alex began to comprehend that beyond the surface-level demands for products or services lay a complex network of emotions, preferences, and unspoken desires that were often the true driving forces behind purchasing decisions. He embarked on a journey to unravel the enigma of human desires, seeking to decode the subtle cues and signals that hinted at the customer's underlying motivations.Through meticulous research and immersive customer interactions, Alex honed his ability to listen intently, to decipher not only what was being said but also to discern the unspoken needs that lingered beneath the surface. He recognized that every customer was unique, with their own set of aspirations, fears, and dreams, and that catering to these individual nuances was the key to forging lasting and meaningful connections.Armed with this newfound understanding, Alex tailored his approach to each customer interaction, abandoning the one-size-fits-all sales pitch in favor of a personalized and empathetic engagement that resonated with the specific desires of his clientele. He embraced the art of active listening, probing beyond the explicit requirements to unravel the implicit aspirations that stirred within the hearts of his prospects.Moreover, Alex realized that anticipating customer needs was just as crucial as understanding their current demands. He adopted a proactive approach, preemptively identifying potential pain points and offering solutions before they even arose. By demonstrating a genuine concern for the well-being and success of his clients, he cultivated a sense of trust and reliability that set him apart from his competitors.In the wake of this profound shift in perspective, Alex witnessed a remarkable transformation in his sales figures. His clients not only returned for repeat business but also became advocates for his services, spreading positive word-of-mouth and solidifying his reputation as a trusted advisor in the industry. The bonds he forged with his customers transcended the realm of mere transactions, evolving into enduring partnerships founded on mutual respect and a shared commitment to mutual growth and success.As the chapter drew to a close, Alex recognized that understanding customer needs was not just about closing a deal; it was about fostering genuine connections, nurturing long-term relationships, and becoming a trusted ally in the pursuit of his customers' aspirations. He realized that by aligning his objectives with the fundamental desires of his clientele, he could not only achieve professional success but also make a meaningful impact on the lives of those he served.

Chapter 4:

EXPLORING THE PSYCHOLOGY OF SELLING AND UNDERSTANDING CONSUMER BEHAVIOR

I. UNVEILING THE ENIGMA OF CONSUMER BEHAVIOR

In the labyrinth of the sales industry, Alex Mason found himself delving deeper into the intricate realm of consumer behavior and the intricate psychology that underpinned every purchasing decision. He recognized that behind every transaction lay a complex interplay of emotions, impulses, and cognitive processes that shaped the very essence of consumer behavior.With an insatiable thirst for knowledge,

Alex immersed himself in the study of consumer psychology, seeking to unravel the mysteries that governed the choices and actions of his clientele. He explored the theories of behavioral economics, delving into the cognitive biases and heuristics that influenced the decision-making processes of individuals. Through this exploration, he gained insights into the ways in which human perception, judgment, and decision-making were inherently susceptible to various cognitive traps and subconscious influences.Alex familiarized himself with the concept of emotional intelligence, understanding that the ability to empathize with the emotions and experiences of his customers was an indispensable tool in his arsenal. He learned to tap into the emotional triggers that could sway a customer's decision, recognizing that the art of selling was as much about appealing to the heart as it was about addressing the mind.Furthermore, Alex unraveled the complexities of social psychology, recognizing the profound impact of social influences, peer pressure, and societal norms on consumer behavior. He understood that the dynamics of social proof, conformity, and social identity played a pivotal role in shaping the preferences and choices of his target audience. By leveraging the power of social validation and community affiliation, he was able to create a sense of belonging and camaraderie that resonated deeply with his clientele.As he navigated the depths of consumer behavior, Alex also delved into the realm of decision-making processes, dissecting the dichotomy between rational and emotional choices. He recognized that while logic and reasoning governed some aspects of consumer decisions, it was often the emotional appeal that tipped the scales in favor of a particular product or service. By aligning his sales strategies with the emotional needs and desires of his customers, he was able to craft compelling narratives that struck a chord and elicited a powerful response.Through this exploration of the intricate web of consumer behavior, Alex gained a profound appreciation for the nuances of human nature and the subtle influences that shaped the choices of his clientele. He recognized that the key to successful selling lay not only in understanding the product but also in deciphering the intricate thought processes and emotional triggers that guided the customer along the path to purchase.As the chapter drew to a close, Alex realized that the mastery of consumer psychology was a never-ending journey, one that demanded constant vigilance, adaptability, and a keen awareness of the evolving trends and influences that shaped the ever-changing landscape of consumer behavior. He understood that by harnessing the power of psychological insights, he could not only predict consumer trends but also influence them, positioning himself as a trailblazer in the realm of sales innovation and customer-centric engagement.

Chapter 5:

DEVELOPING EFFECTIVE COMMUNICATION SKILLS TO ENGAGE AND PERSUADE CUSTOMERS.

I. THE ART OF PERSUASION THROUGH MASTERFUL COMMUNICATION

In the fast-paced world of sales, Alex Mason recognized that effective communication was the cornerstone of success. He understood that the ability to articulate ideas persuasively and engage customers on a profound level was an indispensable skill that could make or break a deal. With this realization firmly entrenched in his mind, Alex embarked on a journey to refine his communication skills, seeking to master the art of crafting compelling narratives and delivering impactful messages that resonated with his audience.He began by honing his verbal communication, recognizing the power of articulating ideas with clarity, confidence, and conviction. Alex learned to structure his conversations in a manner that captured the attention of his customers from the very first word, weaving a narrative that not only highlighted the benefits of his products or services but also catered to the specific needs and desires of his audience. He cultivated the art of storytelling, using vivid imagery and relatable anecdotes to create an emotional connection that left a lasting impression on his listeners.Moreover, Alex delved into the realm of non-verbal communication, recognizing that body language, gestures, and facial expressions played an equally crucial role in conveying trustworthiness and establishing rapport. He learned to project a confident and approachable demeanor, maintaining eye contact, adopting open and welcoming postures, and mirroring the gestures of his customers to foster a sense of familiarity and camaraderie. By mastering the nuances of non-verbal cues, he was able to build an aura of credibility and authenticity that resonated with his clientele.In addition to verbal and non-verbal communication, Alex also delved into the realm of written communication, understanding that the art of persuasion extended beyond face-to-face interactions. He delved into the intricacies of crafting compelling sales pitches, emails, and marketing collateral, recognizing the importance of concise and impactful messaging that cut through the noise and captured the attention of his target audience. He learned to tailor his written communication to the specific needs and preferences of his customers, incorporating persuasive language and engaging narratives that compelled action and fostered a sense of urgency.As the chapter progressed, Alex recognized that effective communication was not just about delivering a message; it was about fostering meaningful connections, building trust, and establishing long-term relationships with his customers. He understood that the key to persuasion lay in understanding the unique communication styles of his audience and tailoring his approach to resonate with their specific preferences and sensibilities.As the chapter drew to a close, Alex realized that the mastery of effective communication was an ongoing journey, one that demanded continuous refinement, adaptability, and a keen understanding of the ever-evolving dynamics of human interaction. He recognized that by harnessing the power of persuasive communication, he could not only influence purchasing decisions but also foster a sense of loyalty and advocacy among his clientele, positioning himself as a trusted advisor and a beacon of authenticity in the realm of sales.

Chapter 6:

THE PILLARS OF TRUST

I. CULTIVATING LASTING CLIENT RELATIONSHIPS

In the labyrinth of the sales industry, Alex Mason came to understand that beyond the transactional nature of deals lay the essence of enduring success—building strong relationships with clients founded on trust, integrity, and genuine rapport. He recognized that the cultivation of these relationships was not merely a means to an end but rather the cornerstone of a sustainable and thriving career in sales.Alex began by investing time and effort in truly understanding his clients beyond their business needs. He delved into the nuances of their personal and professional aspirations, their pain points, and their long-term objectives, recognizing that a genuine interest in their success was the foundation upon which lasting relationships were built. He engaged in meaningful conversations, actively listening to their concerns, and offering solutions that were tailored to their unique circumstances.Moreover, Alex realized that transparency and honesty were non-negotiable elements in fostering trust. He was candid about the limitations of his offerings, ensuring that his clients had a comprehensive understanding of both the benefits and the potential challenges they might encounter. He upheld his commitments with unwavering integrity, delivering on promises and going above and beyond to exceed expectations, even when it meant going the extra mile or making sacrifices on his part.Furthermore, Alex acknowledged the importance of consistent and reliable communication in nurturing client relationships. He established regular touchpoints, providing updates on progress, and soliciting feedback to ensure that his clients felt included and valued throughout the entire engagement process. He responded promptly to their queries and concerns, demonstrating a proactive approach that underscored his dedication to their satisfaction and success.In addition to fostering individual relationships, Alex recognized the power of building a strong network of advocates within the organizations he served. He cultivated relationships not only with his direct clients but also with key stakeholders and decision-makers, understanding that a strong support system within the client's organization could facilitate smoother decision-making processes and pave the way for future opportunities and collaborations.As the chapter progressed, Alex witnessed the fruits of his labor, observing how the cultivation of strong client relationships translated into enduring partnerships and a steady stream of referrals and repeat business. He understood that the trust he had established with his clients extended far beyond the confines of the business realm, permeating into a realm of mutual respect, loyalty, and shared success.As the chapter drew to a close, Alex recognized that building strong client relationships was not just about securing deals; it was about fostering a sense of kinship and camaraderie, where clients felt valued, understood, and supported throughout their journey. He understood that by cultivating these pillars of trust, he could not only solidify his position as a trusted advisor but also foster a legacy of enduring success and prosperity within the realm of the sales industry.

Chapter 7:

THE DYNAMICS OF ADAPTATION

I. NAVIGATING MARKET SHIFTS AND CUSTOMER EVOLUTION

In the dynamic landscape of the sales industry, Alex Mason came face to face with the undeniable reality of ever-shifting market trends and evolving customer preferences. He realized that the ability to adapt swiftly and effectively to these changes was a critical determinant of long-term success and resilience in the face of uncertainty. With this understanding firmly entrenched in his mind, Alex embarked on a journey to master the art of navigating market shifts and anticipating the evolving needs of his clientele.He began by immersing himself in the world of market research, meticulously analyzing industry trends, consumer behavior patterns, and emerging technologies that shaped the trajectory of the market. He recognized the importance of staying ahead of the curve, anticipating changes before they materialized, and proactively adjusting his sales strategies to align with the evolving landscape. By harnessing the power of data-driven insights, he was able to make informed decisions that positioned him as an agile and forward-thinking leader in the industry.Moreover, Alex embraced a mindset of continuous learning and adaptation, recognizing that complacency was the enemy of progress. He sought out opportunities for professional development, attending industry conferences, workshops, and seminars that exposed him to the latest innovations and best practices in the field. He cultivated a spirit of curiosity and a willingness to embrace change, understanding that by staying abreast of emerging trends and technologies, he could not only meet but also surpass the expectations of his discerning clientele.Furthermore, Alex fostered a culture of innovation within his own organization, encouraging his team to think outside the box and explore unconventional strategies that could disrupt the market and cater to the ever-evolving preferences of their customers. He promoted a collaborative environment that encouraged the exchange of ideas and the exploration of new avenues for growth, fostering a culture of resilience and adaptability that positioned his team as trailblazers in the industry.In addition to adapting to market changes, Alex also recognized the importance of evolving customer preferences. He invested time and resources in understanding the shifting needs and desires of his clientele, recognizing that what may have appealed to them yesterday might not necessarily resonate with them today. He engaged in regular feedback sessions, soliciting input from his customers to gain insights into their evolving expectations and preferences, and using this feedback to tailor his offerings and services accordingly.As the chapter progressed,

Alex witnessed the transformative power of adaptation, observing how his ability to navigate market shifts and anticipate customer evolution not only positioned him as a thought leader in the industry but also solidified his reputation as a reliable and innovative partner in the pursuit of his clients' success.As the chapter drew to a close, Alex understood that the dynamics of adaptation were not just about survival; they were about thriving in the face of change, leveraging every shift as an opportunity for growth and innovation. He recognized that by embracing a mindset of agility and resilience, he could not only stay ahead of the competition but also become a catalyst for transformation within the ever-evolving landscape of the sales industry.

Chapter 8:

THE ART OF CONNECTION

I. UNLEASHING THE POWER OF NETWORKING

In the interconnected realm of the sales industry, Alex Mason came to recognize the pivotal role of networking in fostering professional growth and unlocking a world of opportunity. He understood that building a strong and expansive professional network was not just a means to expand his reach but also a gateway to a realm of knowledge, collaboration, and mutual support that could propel his career to unprecedented heights. With this understanding firmly entrenched in his mind,

Alex embarked on a journey to master the art of connection, exploring the nuances of networking and cultivating a robust ecosystem of industry peers, mentors, and collaborators.He began by immersing himself in industry events, conferences, and networking gatherings, recognizing that these platforms served as fertile ground for fostering meaningful connections with like-minded professionals. He engaged in genuine and authentic conversations, seeking to build rapport and establish a foundation of trust that would serve as the bedrock for future collaborations and partnerships. By immersing himself in these networking opportunities, he not only expanded his knowledge base but also positioned himself as a prominent figure within the industry.Moreover, Alex embraced the power of digital networking, recognizing that the virtual realm provided a vast landscape for cultivating connections beyond geographical boundaries. He leveraged social media platforms, professional networking sites, and online forums to engage with a diverse array of professionals, thought leaders, and influencers who could offer unique perspectives and insights that enriched his understanding of the industry. By harnessing the power of digital networking, he was able to establish a global presence that transcended the limitations of physical proximity, positioning himself as a trailblazer in the digital era of sales.Furthermore, Alex recognized the importance of fostering meaningful relationships within his own organization. He actively collaborated with colleagues, sought out mentorship from seasoned professionals, and provided mentorship to aspiring salespersons, understanding that the exchange of knowledge and expertise within the confines of his own team could foster a culture of continuous learning and innovation. By cultivating a spirit of collaboration and mutual support, he not only nurtured a sense of camaraderie but also bolstered the collective success of his organization as a whole.In addition to nurturing professional relationships, Alex also recognized the importance of giving back to the community. He engaged in philanthropic endeavors, participated in community events, and contributed his time and resources to initiatives that aligned with his personal values and the mission of his organization. By actively participating in community building and social responsibility efforts, he not only forged meaningful connections with individuals outside the realm of sales but also solidified his reputation as a conscientious and socially responsible leader within the industry.As the chapter progressed, Alex witnessed the transformative power of networking, observing how his ability to cultivate and nurture meaningful connections not only expanded his professional horizons but also enriched his personal and intellectual growth. He understood that by building a strong and vibrant professional network, he could not only unlock a world of opportunities but also become a catalyst for change and innovation within the dynamic landscape of the sales industry.

Chapter 9:

THE ALCHEMY OF PERSUASION

I. CRAFTING A COMPELLING SALES PITCH THROUGH THE POWER OF STORYTELLING

In the realm of sales, Alex Mason recognized that a compelling sales pitch was not just a transactional tool but a powerful narrative that could captivate the imagination, stir emotions, and compel action. He understood that mastering the art of storytelling was the key to crafting a sales pitch that resonated deeply with his audience, fostering an emotional connection that transcended the boundaries of a mere transaction. With this understanding firmly entrenched in his mind, Alex embarked on a journey to explore the alchemy of persuasion, delving into the intricacies of storytelling and the profound impact it could wield in the realm of sales.He began by immersing himself in the world of storytelling, recognizing that every successful sales pitch was anchored in a narrative that evoked empathy, curiosity, and a sense of urgency within the audience. He honed his ability to weave compelling narratives that not only highlighted the unique features of his products or services but also addressed the underlying needs and desires of his customers. By infusing his sales pitch with authentic and relatable stories, he was able to create a compelling and memorable experience that left a lasting impression on his listeners.Moreover, Alex recognized the importance of structuring his sales pitch in a manner that resonated with the emotions and aspirations of his audience. He understood that the key to capturing their attention lay in tapping into their desires and fears, their dreams and aspirations, and aligning his narrative with their personal experiences and values. By tailoring his storytelling to address the unique circumstances and challenges faced by his customers, he was able to create a sense of relevance and urgency that compelled them to take action.Furthermore, Alex delved into the nuances of visual storytelling, recognizing that the incorporation of multimedia elements such as images, videos, and interactive presentations could enhance the impact of his sales pitch and create a multi-sensory experience that engaged his audience on a deeper level. By leveraging the power of visual storytelling, he was able to convey complex ideas and concepts in a way that was both compelling and easy to understand, fostering a sense of clarity and resonance that transcended the limitations of mere words.In addition to honing his storytelling skills, Alex also recognized the importance of delivering his sales pitch with confidence and conviction. He practiced his presentation meticulously, refining his delivery to exude an aura of credibility and authority that inspired trust and instilled confidence in his audience. By mastering the art of confident communication, he was able to establish himself as a trusted advisor and an authoritative voice within the industry, positioning himself as a go-to resource for all their sales-related needs.As the chapter progressed, Alex witnessed the transformative power of storytelling, observing how his ability to craft a compelling sales pitch not only captured the attention of his audience but also inspired them to take decisive action. He understood that by infusing his sales pitch with the magic of storytelling, he could not only convey the value of his offerings but also foster a sense of connection and trust that positioned him as a thought leader and a trusted ally in the realm of sales.

Chapter 10:

THE DIGITAL FRONTIER

I. LEVERAGING TECHNOLOGY TO REVOLUTIONIZE SALES STRATEGIES

In the rapidly evolving landscape of the sales industry, Alex Mason came to recognize the transformative power of technology and digital platforms in enhancing sales strategies and expanding market reach. He understood that the integration of technology was no longer just an option but a necessity in staying competitive and relevant within the dynamic digital ecosystem. With this understanding firmly entrenched in his mind, Alex embarked on a journey to explore the limitless possibilities that technology offered, delving into the intricacies of digital innovation and its profound impact on the realm of sales.He began by immersing himself in the world of digital tools and software, recognizing that automation and data analytics could streamline the sales process and provide invaluable insights that could inform strategic decision-making. He integrated customer relationship management (CRM) software into his operations, allowing him to track customer interactions, manage leads, and streamline communication to ensure a seamless and personalized experience for his clientele. By leveraging the power of CRM, he was able to nurture strong and enduring relationships with his customers, fostering a sense of loyalty and advocacy that solidified his position as a trusted advisor in the industry.Moreover, Alex explored the potential of data analytics, recognizing that the analysis of customer data and market trends could provide valuable insights into consumer behavior and preferences, enabling him to tailor his sales strategies to meet the specific needs and demands of his target audience. By harnessing the power of data-driven insights, he was able to make informed decisions that optimized his sales process, identified new market opportunities, and predicted future trends with a high degree of accuracy, positioning him as a trailblazer in the realm of sales innovation and strategy.Furthermore, Alex delved into the realm of digital marketing, recognizing that the integration of search engine optimization (SEO), content marketing, and social media engagement could amplify his market reach and enhance brand visibility within the digital sphere. He curated engaging and informative content that resonated with his target audience, leveraging the power of storytelling and visual elements to create a compelling and immersive digital experience that fostered a sense of connection and authenticity. By adopting a comprehensive digital marketing strategy, he was able to expand his reach beyond geographical boundaries, tapping into a global audience that was eager to engage with his brand and offerings.In addition to digital marketing, Alex also recognized the potential of e-commerce platforms and online marketplaces in broadening his sales horizons and reaching new customer segments. He established a robust online presence, creating a user-friendly and intuitive e-commerce platform that provided a seamless and secure shopping experience for his customers. By embracing the convenience of online sales channels, he was able to tap into a vast market of digital consumers, catering to their evolving preferences and enabling them to access his products or services with just a few clicks, positioning his brand at the forefront of the digital revolution in the sales industry.As the chapter progressed, Alex witnessed the transformative power of technology, observing how the integration of digital platforms and innovative tools not only optimized his sales process but also revolutionized the way he engaged with his customers. He understood that by leveraging the power of technology, he could not only enhance his market reach but also foster a culture of innovation and customer-centricity that positioned him as a frontrunner in the digital era of sales.

Chapter 11:

THE RESILIENCE CODE

I. TRIUMPHING OVER OBJECTIONS AND REJECTION IN THE REALM OF SALES

In the tumultuous terrain of the sales industry, Alex Mason confronted a formidable adversary that tested his mettle and resolve—objections and rejection. He realized that the path to success was fraught with countless obstacles, rejections, and objections that threatened to derail his journey and shatter his confidence. With this understanding firmly entrenched in his mind, Alex embarked on a quest to master the resilience code, exploring the intricacies of overcoming objections and handling rejection with unwavering determination and fortitude.He began by embracing objections as opportunities for growth and learning, recognizing that behind every objection lay a hidden opportunity to address concerns and alleviate doubts that could potentially hinder a successful deal. He listened attentively to the concerns of his clients, acknowledging their perspectives with empathy and understanding, and offering solutions that addressed their specific needs and reservations. By viewing objections as stepping stones toward mutual understanding and collaboration, he was able to foster a sense of trust and credibility that positioned him as a reliable and empathetic partner in the sales process.Moreover, Alex developed a resilience mindset that enabled him to navigate through rejection with unwavering determination and grace. He understood that every rejection was not a reflection of his capabilities but rather a part of the inherent nature of the sales industry. He embraced rejection as a catalyst for self-improvement, using each setback as an opportunity to reflect on his approach, refine his strategies, and emerge stronger and more resilient than before. By cultivating a spirit of perseverance and optimism, he was able to bounce back from rejections with renewed vigor and a sense of purpose that propelled him forward on his journey to success.Furthermore, Alex recognized the importance of maintaining a positive mindset in the face of adversity. He practiced self-care and mindfulness, engaging in activities that rejuvenated his spirit and nurtured his well-being, whether through meditation, exercise, or pursuing hobbies that brought him joy and fulfillment. By prioritizing his emotional and mental health, he was able to cultivate a sense of inner strength and balance that fortified his resilience and equipped him with the mental fortitude to confront challenges with a clear and focused mind.In addition to nurturing his own resilience, Alex also extended support to his team, fostering a culture of camaraderie and mutual encouragement that enabled them to navigate through objections and rejection as a unified and determined force. He provided mentorship and guidance to his colleagues, instilling in them the importance of resilience and perseverance in the face of adversity, and creating a support system that bolstered their confidence and nurtured their professional growth and development.As the chapter progressed, Alex witnessed the transformative power of resilience, observing how the mastery of the resilience code not only fortified his own resolve but also inspired his team to confront challenges with unwavering determination and a spirit of unwavering perseverance. He understood that by overcoming objections and handling rejection with resilience and determination, he could not only weather the storms of the sales industry but also emerge as a beacon of resilience and optimism in the face of adversity.

Chapter 12:

THE PATH TO DISTINCTION

I. DECODING COMPETITORS AND UNVEILING UNIQUE SELLING PROPOSITIONS

In the fiercely competitive landscape of the sales industry, Alex Mason recognized the critical importance of analyzing competitors and identifying unique selling propositions that would set him apart from the crowd. He understood that in order to thrive amidst the sea of competition, he needed to unravel the strategies and offerings of his rivals while simultaneously honing in on his own unique strengths and advantages. With this understanding firmly entrenched in his mind,

Alex embarked on a quest to decode his competitors and unearth the elements that would distinguish his brand and offerings in the eyes of his customers.He began by conducting comprehensive competitor analysis, meticulously studying the products, services, and sales strategies employed by his rivals. He delved into the nuances of their offerings, seeking to understand the unique value propositions that drove their success and the areas where they fell short in meeting the needs and expectations of their customers. By immersing himself in the world of competitive analysis, he was able to gain valuable insights into the market landscape, discern emerging trends, and identify gaps and opportunities that would enable him to position his brand and offerings in a league of their own.Moreover, Alex recognized the importance of self-reflection and introspection in uncovering his own unique selling propositions. He engaged in a comprehensive evaluation of his brand's strengths, values, and core competencies, seeking to identify the elements that set him apart from his competitors and resonated deeply with his target audience. He recognized that his unique selling propositions were not just about the features of his products or services but also about the emotional and experiential benefits that his brand could offer to his customers. By aligning his unique selling propositions with the aspirations and desires of his clientele, he was able to create a compelling and differentiated brand narrative that captured their attention and fostered a sense of loyalty and advocacy.Furthermore, Alex harnessed the power of customer feedback and insights to refine his unique selling propositions, understanding that the perspectives and experiences of his customers provided invaluable guidance in shaping his brand's value propositions and offerings. He engaged in regular feedback sessions, soliciting input from his customers to gain insights into their evolving needs and preferences, and using this feedback to tailor his unique selling propositions to address their specific pain points and aspirations. By placing the customer at the center of his value proposition, he was able to foster a sense of connection and resonance that positioned his brand as a trusted and reliable partner in the pursuit of their goals and aspirations.As the chapter progressed, Alex witnessed the transformative power of uncovering unique selling propositions, observing how the mastery of competitive analysis and self-reflection not only positioned his brand as a frontrunner in the industry but also solidified his reputation as an innovator and a trailblazer in the realm of sales differentiation. He understood that by harnessing the power of unique selling propositions, he could not only carve a distinct niche for his brand but also foster a culture of customer-centricity and innovation that set him apart from his competitors and propelled his brand to unprecedented heights of success.

Chapter 13:

THE PRICE OF VALUE

I. UNVEILING THE ESSENCE OF PRICING STRATEGIES AND VALUE PROPOSITIONS

In the intricate tapestry of the sales industry, Alex Mason came to recognize the profound interplay between pricing strategies and value propositions, understanding that the delicate balance between cost and value was the fulcrum upon which successful deals hinged. He realized that understanding the dynamics of pricing and value was not just about setting a monetary figure but rather about communicating the inherent worth and significance of his offerings to his customers. With this understanding firmly entrenched in his mind, Alex embarked on a journey to unravel the essence of pricing strategies and value propositions, seeking to strike a harmonious chord that resonated with the hearts and minds of his clientele.He began by delving into the nuances of pricing psychology, recognizing that the perception of value was often influenced by factors beyond the mere cost of the product or service. He explored the concepts of price anchoring, bundling, and tiered pricing models, understanding that the strategic presentation of pricing could influence the perceived value of his offerings and incentivize customers to make purchasing decisions that aligned with their budget and expectations. By aligning his pricing strategies with the perceived value of his offerings, he was able to create a sense of equilibrium that fostered a positive and rewarding customer experience.Moreover, Alex recognized the importance of communicating the value proposition of his offerings in a manner that resonated with the needs and aspirations of his customers. He delved into the intricacies of value-based pricing, understanding that the perceived benefits and advantages of his products or services were pivotal in shaping the willingness of his customers to pay for the value they received. He crafted compelling value propositions that highlighted the unique features, benefits, and outcomes that his offerings provided, underscoring the transformative impact they could have on the lives and businesses of his clientele. By aligning his value propositions with the specific pain points and aspirations of his customers, he was able to create a narrative that resonated deeply and compelled action.Furthermore, Alex recognized the importance of transparency and honesty in pricing, understanding that fostering trust and credibility was essential in cultivating lasting and meaningful relationships with his customers. He communicated his pricing strategies with clarity and integrity, ensuring that his customers had a comprehensive understanding of the factors that influenced the cost of his offerings and the value they would receive in return. By upholding transparency in his pricing practices, he was able to foster a sense of trust and reliability that positioned his brand as a beacon of authenticity and credibility in the realm of sales.As the chapter progressed, Alex witnessed the transformative power of pricing strategies and value propositions, observing how the mastery of this delicate balance not only optimized his sales process but also fostered a culture of transparency and customer-centricity that set him apart as a trusted and respected leader in the industry. He understood that by harnessing the power of pricing strategies and value propositions, he could not only communicate the worth of his offerings but also foster a sense of trust and loyalty that positioned his brand as a trusted advisor and a catalyst for success within the competitive landscape of the sales industry.

Chapter 14:

THE HORIZONS OF EXPANSION

I. UNVEILING THE JOURNEY TO AN ENLARGED CUSTOMER BASE AND NEW MARKET FRONTIERS

In the expansive realm of the sales industry, Alex Mason recognized the paramount importance of expanding his customer base and venturing into new market territories as a means of sustaining growth and fostering long-term success. He understood that the pursuit of new customers and markets was not just about numerical expansion but also about cultivating a diversified and resilient ecosystem that could withstand the ebb and flow of market dynamics. With this understanding firmly entrenched in his mind, Alex embarked on a quest to explore the horizons of expansion, seeking to unveil the intricacies of customer acquisition and market penetration that would pave the way for sustained prosperity and growth.He began by conducting comprehensive market research, meticulously analyzing the demographics, behaviors, and preferences of potential customer segments in untapped markets. He identified emerging trends and unmet needs within these market segments, understanding that the key to successful expansion lay in offering tailored solutions that addressed the unique challenges and aspirations of these customer groups. By immersing himself in the world of market research, he was able to gain invaluable insights that informed his expansion strategy, enabling him to position his brand and offerings in a manner that resonated deeply with the aspirations and preferences of his target audience.Moreover, Alex recognized the importance of diversifying his customer acquisition channels, understanding that the pursuit of new markets required a multi-faceted approach that leveraged various sales channels and engagement platforms. He explored the potential of digital marketing, social media engagement, and e-commerce platforms as avenues to reach a global audience and engage with customers beyond geographical boundaries. By harnessing the power of digital channels, he was able to expand his reach and tap into a vast market of digital consumers who were eager to explore and engage with his brand and offerings.Furthermore, Alex cultivated strategic partnerships and alliances with local businesses and industry players in new markets, understanding that collaboration was a powerful tool in gaining a foothold in uncharted territories. He fostered a spirit of camaraderie and mutual support, forging alliances that enabled him to leverage the expertise and market insights of local partners while simultaneously introducing his brand and offerings to their existing customer base. By nurturing strategic partnerships, he was able to establish a strong presence in new markets and cultivate a sense of trust and credibility that positioned his brand as a reliable and valued partner within these ecosystems.In addition to customer acquisition, Alex also recognized the importance of fostering customer loyalty and advocacy as a means of sustaining growth and prosperity in new markets. He implemented comprehensive customer retention strategies, offering personalized and exceptional customer experiences that fostered a sense of loyalty and advocacy among his clientele. He engaged in regular communication and feedback sessions, seeking input from his customers to understand their evolving needs and preferences, and using this feedback to tailor his offerings and services to meet their expectations. By prioritizing customer satisfaction and engagement, he was able to foster a loyal customer base that not only sustained his growth but also served as ambassadors for his brand within the new markets he ventured into.As the chapter progressed, Alex witnessed the transformative power of expanding his customer base and reaching new markets, observing how the mastery of this strategy not only diversified his revenue streams but also solidified his position as an industry leader with a global footprint. He understood that by harnessing the potential of new markets, he could not only drive growth and prosperity for his brand but also foster a culture of innovation and customer-centricity that positioned him as a trailblazer in the dynamic and ever-evolving landscape of the sales industry.

Chapter 15:

THE SYMPHONY OF PROMOTION

I. ORCHESTRATING EFFECTIVE MARKETING TECHNIQUES FOR LASTING IMPACT

In the symphony of the sales industry, Alex Mason recognized the pivotal role of effective marketing techniques and promotional strategies in amplifying brand visibility, driving customer engagement, and fostering long-term brand loyalty. He understood that the implementation of a comprehensive and targeted marketing strategy was not just about generating buzz but also about nurturing meaningful and enduring relationships with his customers. With this understanding firmly entrenched in his mind,

Alex embarked on a journey to master the art of promotion, delving into the intricacies of marketing techniques and strategies that would resonate deeply with his target audience and position his brand as a frontrunner in the industry.He began by cultivating a deep understanding of his target audience, recognizing that effective marketing was not just about reaching a wide audience but rather about engaging with the right audience with tailored messages and offerings that addressed their unique needs and aspirations. He conducted comprehensive market research, delving into the demographics, behaviors, and preferences of his target audience, and using this information to craft personalized marketing messages and campaigns that resonated deeply with their desires and values. By tailoring his marketing techniques to the specific needs of his audience, he was able to create a sense of relevance and resonance that fostered a strong and enduring connection with his customers.Moreover, Alex recognized the power of integrated marketing campaigns that leveraged multiple channels and touchpoints to engage with his audience at various stages of the customer journey. He integrated the use of digital marketing, social media engagement, content marketing, and traditional advertising to create a cohesive and immersive brand experience that left a lasting impression on his customers. By orchestrating an integrated marketing strategy, he was able to amplify his brand visibility and drive customer engagement across multiple platforms, ensuring that his brand remained top-of-mind among his target audience.Furthermore, Alex harnessed the power of storytelling in his marketing campaigns, recognizing that the incorporation of compelling narratives and authentic experiences could create an emotional connection that resonated deeply with his audience. He crafted engaging and immersive content that conveyed the essence of his brand and offerings, using storytelling as a vehicle to communicate the values, vision, and mission that underpinned his brand's identity. By infusing his marketing campaigns with the magic of storytelling, he was able to foster a sense of authenticity and trust that positioned his brand as more than just a product or service but rather as a trusted partner and advisor in the pursuit of his customers' goals and aspirations.In addition to storytelling, Alex also recognized the importance of measuring the effectiveness of his marketing campaigns through key performance indicators (KPIs) and analytics. He monitored the performance of his campaigns in real-time, analyzing metrics such as customer engagement, conversion rates, and return on investment (ROI) to gauge the impact and success of his marketing initiatives. By leveraging the power of data-driven insights, he was able to make informed decisions that optimized his marketing strategies and ensured that every marketing dollar was spent with maximum impact and efficacy.As the chapter progressed, Alex witnessed the transformative power of effective marketing techniques and promotional strategies, observing how the mastery of this art not only amplified his brand presence but also fostered a culture of customer-centricity and innovation that positioned his brand as a trailblazer in the competitive landscape of the sales industry. He understood that by harnessing the potential of effective marketing, he could not only engage with his audience on a deeper level but also foster a legacy of enduring trust and loyalty that transcended the confines of traditional marketing practices and propelled his brand to unprecedented heights of success.

Chapter 16:

THE PILLARS OF CONSISTENCY

I. SUSTAINING PRODUCT QUALITY AND SERVICE EXCELLENCE FOR LASTING CUSTOMER TRUST

In the bedrock of the sales industry, Alex Mason recognized the indispensable role of maintaining consistency in product quality and service delivery as the cornerstone of building enduring customer trust and loyalty. He understood that the assurance of consistent excellence was not just about meeting expectations but also about surpassing them with every interaction and transaction. With this understanding firmly entrenched in his mind, Alex embarked on a journey to establish the pillars of consistency, delving into the intricacies of quality management and service excellence that would lay the foundation for a legacy of enduring customer satisfaction and advocacy.He began by cultivating a culture of quality within his organization, recognizing that consistent product quality was not just a result of stringent quality control measures but also a reflection of a commitment to excellence that permeated every aspect of his business operations. He implemented robust quality control processes that ensured every product met the highest standards of craftsmanship and durability, leaving no room for compromise or deviation from the established benchmarks of quality. By instilling a culture of excellence within his team, he was able to foster a sense of pride and ownership that translated into products of unparalleled quality and value for his customers.Moreover, Alex recognized the importance of delivering consistent service excellence that complemented the superior quality of his products. He implemented comprehensive training programs for his customer-facing staff, equipping them with the skills and knowledge necessary to provide personalized and exceptional service experiences that exceeded the expectations of his customers. He emphasized the importance of empathy and understanding in customer interactions, empowering his team to anticipate and address the unique needs and preferences of each customer with a level of care and attention that fostered a sense of trust and satisfaction.Furthermore, Alex embraced the power of feedback and continuous improvement in maintaining consistency in product quality and service delivery. He solicited regular feedback from his customers, seeking insights into their experiences and using this information to identify areas for improvement and innovation. He implemented a cycle of continuous improvement that enabled him to refine his products and services based on the evolving needs and preferences of his customers, ensuring that every interaction and transaction was a testament to his commitment to excellence and customer satisfaction.In addition to customer feedback, Alex also recognized the importance of establishing robust quality assurance protocols that ensured every aspect of his operations adhered to the highest standards of excellence. He implemented comprehensive quality assurance processes that spanned every stage of the production and service delivery cycle, from sourcing raw materials to post-sale support, ensuring that every touchpoint reflected the hallmark of quality and reliability that his customers had come to expect from his brand.As the chapter progressed, Alex witnessed the transformative power of maintaining consistency in product quality and service delivery, observing how the mastery of this practice not only fostered enduring customer trust and loyalty but also solidified his brand's reputation as a symbol of excellence and reliability within the sales industry. He understood that by upholding the pillars of consistency, he could not only meet but also exceed the expectations of his customers, fostering a legacy of enduring trust and advocacy that positioned his brand as a

beacon of unwavering quality and service
excellence in the competitive landscape of the
sales industry.

Chapter 17:

THE TRAIL OF ASSURANCE

I. CRAFTING A ROBUST FOLLOW-UP PROCESS FOR LASTING CUSTOMER SATISFACTION AND RETENTION

In the fabric of the sales industry, Alex Mason recognized the pivotal role of developing a strong follow-up process as a means of ensuring lasting customer satisfaction and fostering enduring brand loyalty. He understood that the journey to customer satisfaction did not end with the completion of a transaction but rather extended beyond to encompass a comprehensive and attentive post-sale engagement that nurtured a sense of trust and reassurance among his clientele. With this understanding firmly entrenched in his mind, Alex embarked on a quest to craft a robust follow-up process, delving into the intricacies of customer engagement and relationship management that would pave the way for a legacy of enduring customer satisfaction and retention.He began by implementing a comprehensive post-sale engagement strategy that encompassed regular communication and feedback sessions with his customers. He reached out to his customers after every transaction, seeking their input and insights into their experiences, and using this feedback to gauge their satisfaction levels and identify areas for improvement and refinement. By fostering an open line of communication, he was able to demonstrate his commitment to their satisfaction and establish a sense of rapport and trust that transcended the boundaries of mere business transactions.Moreover, Alex recognized the importance of personalized follow-up engagements that addressed the unique needs and preferences of each customer. He tailored his post-sale communications to reflect the specific products or services purchased by his customers, offering personalized recommendations, and support that added value to their overall experience. He acknowledged their loyalty and support, expressing his gratitude through personalized messages and gestures that fostered a sense of connection and appreciation among his clientele.Furthermore, Alex leveraged the power of technology and automation in streamlining his follow-up process, ensuring that no customer interaction or feedback went unnoticed or unaddressed. He implemented customer relationship management (CRM) software that enabled him to track customer interactions, manage follow-up engagements, and analyze customer feedback in a systematic and organized manner. By harnessing the power of automation, he was able to streamline his follow-up process and ensure that every customer received the attention and support they deserved, fostering a sense of satisfaction and reassurance that solidified their loyalty and advocacy for his brand.In addition to automated follow-up processes, Alex also recognized the importance of proactive customer support and assistance that went above and beyond the standard post-sale engagement. He established a dedicated customer support team that was readily available to address any queries, concerns, or issues that his customers may encounter, providing timely and effective solutions that reflected his commitment to their satisfaction and well-being. By offering proactive customer support, he was able to foster a culture of trust and reliability that positioned his brand as a dependable and valued partner in the pursuit of his customers' goals and aspirations.As the chapter progressed, Alex witnessed the transformative power of a robust follow-up process, observing how the mastery of this practice not only fostered lasting customer satisfaction but also solidified his brand's reputation as a trusted and attentive advisor within the sales industry. He understood that by nurturing a strong follow-up process, he could not only cultivate enduring customer relationships but also foster a legacy of trust and loyalty that positioned his brand as a beacon of

assurance and support in the competitive
landscape of the sales industry.

Chapter 18:

THE ART OF LEADERSHIP

I. NURTURING A DYNAMIC SALES TEAM AND CULTIVATING A CULTURE OF SUCCESS AND MOTIVATION

In the dynamic realm of the sales industry, Alex Mason recognized the paramount importance of effective leadership in managing a sales team and fostering a culture of success and motivation. He understood that the success of his team was not just a reflection of their individual capabilities but also a testament to the strength of the leadership and the culture of empowerment and inspiration that permeated every aspect of their work. With this understanding firmly entrenched in his mind, Alex embarked on a journey to master the art of leadership, delving into the intricacies of team management and motivation that would pave the way for a legacy of enduring success and growth within his organization.He began by cultivating a culture of open communication and transparency within his team, recognizing that fostering a sense of trust and collaboration was essential in nurturing a cohesive and high-performing team. He encouraged open dialogue and feedback sessions, providing his team members with a platform to express their ideas, concerns, and aspirations freely. By promoting a culture of open communication, he was able to foster a sense of camaraderie and shared purpose among his team members, instilling a spirit of unity and mutual support that propelled them toward their collective goals and aspirations.Moreover, Alex recognized the importance of setting clear goals and expectations for his team, providing them with a roadmap to success that outlined the key performance indicators and milestones they were expected to achieve. He engaged his team members in the goal-setting process, seeking their input and insights into the development of the team's objectives and strategies. By involving his team in the goal-setting process, he was able to foster a sense of ownership and accountability that motivated them to go above and beyond in their pursuit of excellence and success.Furthermore, Alex invested in the professional development and growth of his team members, understanding that fostering a culture of continuous learning and improvement was essential in nurturing a high-performing and motivated workforce. He provided his team with access to comprehensive training programs, workshops, and mentorship opportunities that enabled them to enhance their skills and expertise in the realm of sales. By prioritizing the professional development of his team members, he was able to cultivate a culture of innovation and excellence that positioned his team as thought leaders and trailblazers in the sales industry.In addition to professional development, Alex recognized the importance of celebrating achievements and milestones within his team, fostering a culture of recognition and appreciation that motivated his team members to strive for excellence and success. He acknowledged their efforts and accomplishments through regular recognition programs, awards, and incentives that highlighted their contributions and dedication to the success of the organization. By celebrating achievements, he was able to foster a culture of motivation and engagement that inspired his team members to reach new heights of success and innovation within their roles.As the chapter progressed, Alex witnessed the transformative power of effective team management and leadership, observing how the mastery of this art not only fostered a culture of success and motivation but also solidified his position as a respected and inspirational leader within the sales industry. He understood that by nurturing a dynamic sales team and fostering a culture of empowerment and motivation, he could not only drive growth and success within his organization but also inspire a legacy of excellence and innovation that positioned his team as a beacon of success and motivation in the competitive landscape of the sales industry.

Chapter 19:

THE FEEDBACK LOOP

I. HARNESSING CUSTOMER INPUT FOR CONTINUOUS IMPROVEMENT AND INNOVATION

In the interconnected web of the sales industry, Alex Mason recognized the pivotal role of customer feedback in driving continuous improvement and fostering innovation within his organization. He understood that the voices of his customers were not just a source of input but also a wellspring of invaluable insights and perspectives that could inform strategic decision-making and shape the trajectory of his business. With this understanding firmly entrenched in his mind, Alex embarked on a quest to harness the power of customer feedback, delving into the intricacies of feedback analysis and implementation that would pave the way for a legacy of enduring customer satisfaction and innovation within his organization.He began by establishing a comprehensive feedback collection system that enabled him to gather input from his customers at various touchpoints along their journey. He solicited feedback through surveys, reviews, and direct interactions, providing his customers with multiple channels through which they could express their opinions, suggestions, and concerns. By establishing a robust feedback collection system, he was able to create a platform for his customers to voice their experiences and expectations, fostering a sense of empowerment and partnership that positioned them as stakeholders in the evolution and improvement of his offerings.Moreover, Alex recognized the importance of analyzing customer feedback in a systematic and structured manner, understanding that the extraction of meaningful insights from customer input required a comprehensive and analytical approach. He implemented data analytics and sentiment analysis tools that enabled him to identify patterns, trends, and sentiments within the feedback provided by his customers. By leveraging the power of data-driven insights, he was able to gain a comprehensive understanding of the evolving needs and preferences of his customers, enabling him to make informed decisions that aligned with their expectations and aspirations.Furthermore, Alex fostered a culture of responsiveness and agility in addressing customer feedback, understanding that timely and effective responses were essential in fostering a sense of trust and reliability among his clientele. He established a dedicated customer support team that was readily available to address any queries, concerns, or issues that his customers may encounter, providing personalized and effective solutions that reflected his commitment to their satisfaction and well-being. By prioritizing responsiveness, he was able to foster a culture of customer-centricity that positioned his organization as a reliable and valued partner in the pursuit of his customers' goals and aspirations.In addition to responsiveness, Alex also recognized the importance of implementing a structured feedback implementation process that translated customer insights into tangible actions and improvements within his organization. He engaged his cross-functional teams in regular feedback review sessions, leveraging their expertise and insights to identify actionable strategies and initiatives that would address the concerns and suggestions provided by their customers. By implementing a structured feedback implementation process, he was able to foster a culture of continuous improvement and innovation that positioned his organization as a pioneer in the realm of customer-centricity and responsiveness within the sales industry.As the chapter progressed, Alex witnessed the transformative power of customer feedback, observing how the mastery of this practice not only drove continuous improvement but also fostered a culture of customer-centricity and innovation that positioned his organization as a trusted and respected leader within the sales industry. He understood that by harnessing the power of customer feedback, he could not only meet but also exceed the expectations of his customers, fostering a legacy of enduring trust and loyalty that transcended the confines of traditional business practices and propelled his organization to unprecedented heights of success and innovation.

Chapter 20:

THE TIME EQUATION

I. UNRAVELING THE SIGNIFICANCE OF TIME MANAGEMENT AND PRODUCTIVITY IN THE ART OF SALES

In the intricate tapestry of the sales industry, Alex Mason recognized the paramount importance of time management and productivity as the bedrock upon which successful sales strategies were built. He understood that in the fast-paced and dynamic landscape of the sales industry, the efficient allocation of time and resources was not just a necessity but also a strategic advantage that could propel him toward unprecedented levels of success and growth. With this understanding firmly entrenched in his mind, Alex embarked on a journey to unravel the significance of time management and productivity, delving into the intricacies of efficient resource allocation and workflow optimization that would position him as a trailblazer in the realm of sales excellence.He began by cultivating a disciplined approach to time management, recognizing that effective time allocation was not just about working harder but also about working smarter. He implemented comprehensive time management techniques that enabled him to prioritize tasks, set achievable goals, and allocate resources in a manner that optimized productivity and minimized wastage. By embracing a disciplined approach to time management, he was able to streamline his workflow and focus his energy on high-impact activities that drove tangible results and propelled him toward his sales targets and objectives.Moreover, Alex recognized the importance of setting realistic and achievable targets that aligned with his long-term goals and aspirations. He established a structured goal-setting process that encompassed short-term, medium-term, and long-term objectives, providing him with a roadmap to success that delineated the milestones and key performance indicators he needed to achieve. By aligning his time management strategies with his defined goals, he was able to create a sense of purpose and direction that guided his actions and decisions, ensuring that every minute of his time was spent in pursuit of meaningful and impactful outcomes.Furthermore, Alex harnessed the power of technology and automation in optimizing his productivity and time management practices. He leveraged advanced sales management software and productivity tools that enabled him to streamline his administrative tasks, automate routine processes, and gain real-time insights into his sales performance and progress. By harnessing the power of technology, he was able to free up valuable time that could be invested in high-value activities, such as customer engagement, relationship building, and strategic planning, that drove tangible results and fostered enduring customer satisfaction and loyalty.In addition to technology, Alex recognized the importance of fostering a culture of productivity and accountability within his organization. He empowered his team members with the tools and resources necessary to optimize their time and workflow, encouraging them to embrace a proactive and results-driven approach to their tasks and responsibilities. He fostered a culture of collaboration and mutual support, providing his team with the guidance and mentorship necessary to enhance their productivity and achieve their individual and collective goals. By fostering a culture of productivity, he was able to create a dynamic and high-performing team that not only met but also exceeded the expectations of their customers and the organization.As the chapter progressed, Alex witnessed the transformative power of time management and productivity, observing how the mastery of this art not only optimized his sales process but also fostered a culture of efficiency and excellence that positioned him as a respected and inspirational leader within the sales industry. He understood that by harnessing the potential of time management and productivity, he could not only maximize his sales potential but also foster a legacy of enduring success and innovation that positioned him as a beacon of efficiency and excellence in the competitive landscape of the sales industry.

Chapter 21:

THE BALANCE EQUATION

I. CONQUERING BURNOUT AND NURTURING A HEALTHY WORK-LIFE HARMONY IN THE REALM OF SALES

In the demanding terrain of the sales industry, Alex Mason recognized the critical importance of overcoming burnout and maintaining a healthy work-life balance as the key to sustaining long-term success and well-being. He understood that the relentless pursuit of professional excellence could often come at the cost of personal health and fulfillment, and that the cultivation of a harmonious balance between

work and life was essential in fostering a sense
of well-being and satisfaction that extended
beyond the confines of the workplace. With this
understanding firmly entrenched in his mind,
Alex embarked on a quest to conquer burnout
and nurture a healthy work-life harmony,
delving into the intricacies of stress management
and holistic well-being that would position him
as a champion of sustainable success and
fulfillment within the sales industry.He began by
acknowledging the signs and symptoms of
burnout, recognizing that the early identification
and management of stress were essential in
preventing the onset of burnout and its
detrimental effects on his physical and mental
well-being. He cultivated self-awareness and
mindfulness, seeking to understand the triggers
and stressors that contributed to his feelings of
exhaustion and overwhelm, and using this
awareness to implement proactive stress
management techniques that fostered a sense of
balance and resilience within his daily
life.Moreover, Alex prioritized the cultivation of
a healthy work-life balance that encompassed

not just his professional responsibilities but also his personal passions, relationships, and well-being. He established clear boundaries between his work and personal life, allocating dedicated time for self-care, relaxation, and meaningful interactions with his loved ones. By embracing a holistic approach to well-being, he was able to create a sense of harmony and fulfillment that transcended the confines of professional success and positioned him as a role model for sustainable and balanced living within the sales industry.Furthermore, Alex leveraged the power of time management and priority setting in optimizing his work-life balance. He implemented effective time management techniques that enabled him to allocate dedicated time for work, leisure, and personal pursuits, ensuring that every aspect of his life received the attention and care it deserved. He set realistic and achievable goals that aligned with his values and aspirations, fostering a sense of purpose and fulfillment that guided his actions and decisions in both his professional and personal endeavors.In addition to time management, Alex recognized the importance of incorporating regular physical exercise and healthy lifestyle practices into his daily routine. He prioritized regular exercise, adequate sleep, and nutritious eating habits, understanding that a healthy body was essential in fostering a resilient and balanced mind. He engaged in activities that rejuvenated his spirit and revitalized his energy, such as meditation, yoga, and outdoor recreation, that fostered a sense of tranquility and well-being that positioned him as a beacon of holistic health and vitality within the competitive landscape of the sales industry.As the chapter progressed, Alex witnessed the transformative power of conquering burnout and nurturing a healthy work-life harmony, observing how the mastery of this practice not only optimized his personal well-being but also fostered a culture of balance and fulfillment within his organization. He understood that by prioritizing his well-being and embracing a holistic approach to life, he could not only sustain his success but also inspire a legacy of well-being and resilience that transcended the confines of professional achievements and positioned him as a trailblazer for holistic success and fulfillment within the competitive and demanding landscape of the sales industry.

Chapter 22:

THE LEARNING ODYSSEY

I. EMPHASIZING THE SIGNIFICANCE OF CONTINUOUS GROWTH AND PERSONAL DEVELOPMENT IN THE SALES JOURNEY

In the ever-evolving landscape of the sales industry, Alex Mason recognized the pivotal importance of continuous learning and personal development as the driving force behind professional growth and sustainable success. He understood that the pursuit of excellence was not just a destination but rather a lifelong journey of discovery, learning, and self-improvement that propelled him toward unprecedented levels of mastery and innovation within his field. With this understanding firmly entrenched in his mind, Alex embarked on an odyssey of learning, delving into the intricacies of personal development and continuous education that would position him as a champion of lifelong growth and success within the sales industry.He began by cultivating a thirst for knowledge and a passion for learning that transcended the confines of his professional responsibilities. He embraced a mindset of curiosity and exploration, seeking to expand his horizons and deepen his understanding of the principles and practices that underpinned the sales industry. He engaged in regular reading, research, and networking, immersing himself in a world of diverse perspectives and insights that broadened his intellectual prowess and enriched his understanding of the ever-evolving dynamics of the sales landscape.Moreover, Alex recognized the transformative power of formal education and professional certifications in enhancing his expertise and credibility within the sales industry. He pursued advanced courses, workshops, and certifications that enabled him to acquire specialized knowledge and skills in areas such as sales techniques, customer relationship management, and market analysis. By investing in formal education, he was able to position himself as a thought leader and expert within his field, garnering the respect and admiration of his peers and clientele and solidifying his reputation as a trailblazer in the realm of sales excellence and innovation.Furthermore, Alex harnessed the power of mentorship and guidance in nurturing his personal and professional development. He sought the mentorship of seasoned professionals and industry leaders who had achieved significant milestones and successes within the sales industry, leveraging their insights and experiences to navigate the complexities and challenges of his own career journey. He engaged in regular mentorship sessions, seeking guidance and advice on key decisions and strategies that shaped his professional trajectory and positioned him for long-term growth and success within the competitive landscape of the sales industry.In addition to formal education and mentorship, Alex recognized the importance of embracing a culture of continuous improvement and self-reflection in nurturing his personal development. He engaged in regular self-assessments and feedback sessions, seeking to identify areas for improvement and refinement within his skill set and mindset. He embraced constructive criticism and feedback as opportunities for growth and transformation, using this input to set actionable goals and strategies that enabled him to overcome his limitations and reach new heights of personal and professional excellence within his career.As the chapter progressed, Alex witnessed the transformative power of continuous learning and personal development, observing how the mastery of this practice not only enhanced his expertise but also fostered a culture of innovation and resilience within his organization. He understood that by prioritizing his personal growth and embracing a culture of continuous learning, he could not only elevate his professional standing but also inspire a legacy of excellence and innovation that transcended the confines of traditional career trajectories and positioned him as a beacon of lifelong growth and success within the competitive and ever-evolving landscape of the sales industry.

Chapter 23:

THE RESILIENCE MANDATE

I. NAVIGATING ECONOMIC CHALLENGES AND MARKET FLUCTUATIONS IN THE SALES LANDSCAPE

In the dynamic realm of the sales industry, Alex Mason recognized the critical importance of resilience and adaptability in navigating through economic challenges and market fluctuations. He understood that the sales landscape was inherently susceptible to the ebbs and flows of the global economy and that the ability to weather turbulent market conditions was essential in sustaining long-term success and growth within his organization. With this understanding firmly entrenched in his mind, Alex embarked on a journey of resilience, delving into the intricacies of market analysis and strategic planning that would position him as a champion of adaptability and foresight within the sales industry.He began by cultivating a comprehensive understanding of the economic forces and market trends that shaped the dynamics of the sales landscape. He engaged in regular market analysis and research, seeking to identify emerging patterns and shifts in consumer behavior and market demand that could impact the performance and growth of his business. He monitored key economic indicators, such as inflation rates, interest rates, and consumer spending patterns, that provided insights into the overall health and stability of the market. By staying informed and vigilant, he was able to anticipate potential challenges and proactively develop strategies and contingency plans that mitigated the impact of economic downturns and market fluctuations on his business.Moreover, Alex embraced the power of strategic planning and risk management in navigating through economic challenges and market uncertainties. He established a comprehensive risk management framework that identified potential threats and vulnerabilities within his business operations, and implemented proactive measures to mitigate their impact on his organization. He diversified his product offerings and customer segments, reducing his reliance on specific market niches or product categories that were susceptible to economic volatility. By embracing a proactive approach to risk management, he was able to build a resilient and adaptable business model that withstood the tests of economic challenges and market uncertainties.Furthermore, Alex recognized the importance of fostering a culture of innovation and agility within his organization. He empowered his team members to think creatively and embrace change as an opportunity for growth and transformation. He encouraged the exploration of new market segments, product innovations, and sales strategies that enabled his organization to pivot and adapt to the evolving demands and preferences of their customers. By fostering a culture of innovation and agility, he was able to position his organization as a pioneer in the realm of adaptive sales strategies and market resilience, ensuring that they remained competitive and resilient in the face of economic challenges and market fluctuations.In addition to innovation, Alex leveraged the power of strategic partnerships and collaborations in strengthening his organization's resilience and adaptability. He forged strategic alliances with key industry players and stakeholders, leveraging their expertise and resources to navigate through challenging economic climates and market uncertainties. He engaged in collaborative initiatives and joint ventures that enabled his organization to access new markets, technologies, and distribution channels, diversifying their revenue streams and fortifying their position against the volatility of the market. By fostering strategic partnerships, he was able to build a network of support and resilience that positioned his organization as a formidable player in the face of economic challenges and market fluctuations.As the chapter progressed, Alex witnessed the transformative power of resilience and adaptability, observing how the mastery of these traits not only enabled his organization to withstand economic challenges but also fostered a culture of innovation and foresight that positioned them as trailblazers in the sales industry. He understood that by prioritizing resilience and adaptability, he could not only navigate through market fluctuations but also inspire a legacy of agility and foresight that transcended the confines of traditional business practices and positioned his organization as a beacon of resilience and innovation within the competitive and ever-evolving landscape of the sales industry.

Chapter 24:

THE EXPANSION FRONTIER

I. DIVERSIFYING SALES CHANNELS AND EMBRACING NEW AVENUES FOR SUSTAINABLE GROWTH

In the expansive realm of the sales industry, Alex Mason recognized the critical importance of diversifying sales channels and exploring new opportunities for sustainable growth. He understood that the pursuit of long-term success was not just confined to traditional sales avenues but also encompassed the exploration of innovative and diverse channels that could expand the reach and impact of his business. With this understanding firmly entrenched in his mind, Alex embarked on an exploration of the expansion frontier, delving into the intricacies of market diversification and strategic expansion that would position him as a pioneer of sustainable growth and innovation within the sales industry.He began by conducting comprehensive market research and analysis to identify emerging trends and consumer preferences that could inform his sales channel diversification strategy. He sought to understand the evolving needs and preferences of his target audience, and to identify the channels and platforms that resonated most with their purchasing behaviors and communication preferences. By gaining insights into the dynamics of the market, he was able to develop a strategic roadmap for channel diversification that leveraged the power of multiple touchpoints to reach and engage his audience effectively.Moreover, Alex recognized the transformative power of e-commerce and digital platforms in expanding his sales channels and reaching new markets. He invested in the development of a robust online presence, establishing an e-commerce platform that enabled his customers to access his products and services conveniently and securely from anywhere in the world. He optimized his website for user experience and search engine visibility, ensuring that it provided a seamless and intuitive interface that facilitated easy navigation and transaction processing. By embracing e-commerce, he was able to tap into a global audience and expand his market reach beyond the confines of traditional brick-and-mortar operations, positioning his business for unprecedented growth and success in the digital age.Furthermore, Alex leveraged the power of strategic partnerships and collaborations in diversifying his sales channels and exploring new opportunities for growth. He forged alliances with complementary businesses and industry stakeholders, leveraging their expertise and resources to access new markets, technologies, and distribution channels. He engaged in joint marketing campaigns and cross-promotional activities that amplified his brand visibility and market presence, positioning his business as a formidable player in the realm of strategic sales channel diversification and sustainable growth.In addition to e-commerce and strategic partnerships, Alex recognized the importance of embracing omni-channel marketing strategies that integrated multiple sales channels into a cohesive and seamless customer experience. He established a unified brand presence across various platforms, including social media, mobile applications, and physical retail outlets, ensuring that every customer touchpoint reflected the core values and messaging of his brand. By embracing omni-channel marketing, he was able to create a holistic and integrated customer journey that fostered engagement and loyalty, positioning his business as a preferred choice for consumers seeking a seamless and personalized shopping experience.As the chapter progressed, Alex witnessed the transformative power of sales channel diversification and market expansion, observing how the mastery of these strategies not only expanded his market reach but also fostered a culture of innovation and agility within his organization. He understood that by

embracing new sales channels and exploring
opportunities for growth, he could not only
expand his market presence but also inspire a
legacy of adaptability and foresight that
positioned his organization as a trailblazer for
sustainable growth and innovation within the
competitive and ever-evolving landscape of the
sales industry.

Chapter 25:

THE JOURNEY TO SUCCESS

I. EMBRACING THE PATH OF EXCELLENCE AND LONG-TERM ACHIEVEMENT IN THE SALES INDUSTRY

In the transformative odyssey of the sales industry, Alex Mason's journey had been a testament to the transformative power of dedication, perseverance, and innovation in the pursuit of long-term success and excellence. Through the trials and triumphs of his career, he had unearthed invaluable insights and principles that had guided him towards unprecedented heights of achievement and recognition within the competitive landscape of the sales industry. As he reflected on his journey, he recognized the critical importance of embracing a holistic approach to sales excellence that encompassed not just the mastery of sales techniques and strategies but also the cultivation of a resilient mindset and an unwavering commitment to customer satisfaction and innovation.Throughout his career, Alex had emphasized the significance of building enduring relationships with his clientele, understanding that the foundation of sustainable success lay in the cultivation of trust, transparency, and integrity within every interaction and transaction. He had prioritized the understanding of his customers' needs and desires, tailoring his sales strategies and approaches to reflect their unique preferences and aspirations. By embracing a customer-centric approach, he had been able to foster enduring loyalty and advocacy within his clientele, positioning his brand as a trusted and reliable partner in their pursuit of success and fulfillment.Moreover, Alex had recognized the transformative power of continuous learning and personal development in fostering his professional growth and expertise within the sales industry. He had embraced a culture of curiosity and exploration, seeking to expand his knowledge and skills through formal education, mentorship, and self-reflection. By prioritizing his personal development, he had been able to position himself as a thought leader and innovator within his field, garnering the respect and admiration of his peers and clientele and solidifying his reputation as a trailblazer for excellence and innovation within the sales industry.Furthermore, Alex had navigated through economic challenges and market fluctuations with resilience and adaptability, understanding that the ability to weather turbulent market conditions was essential in sustaining long-term success and growth within his organization. He had embraced the power of diversifying sales channels and exploring new opportunities for growth, leveraging the potential of e-commerce, strategic partnerships, and omni-channel marketing strategies to expand his market reach and amplify his brand presence. By embracing innovative sales strategies, he had positioned his organization as a pioneer of sustainable growth and market resilience, ensuring that they remained competitive and adaptable in the face of economic challenges and market uncertainties.As he concluded his journey, Alex emphasized the significance of embracing a holistic approach to sales excellence that prioritized customer satisfaction, personal growth, and market resilience. He underscored the importance of perseverance and adaptability in the face of challenges and uncertainties, recognizing that the pursuit of long-term success required a steadfast commitment to excellence and innovation. He encouraged aspiring sales professionals to embrace the transformative power of dedication, perseverance, and innovation in their own journeys, understanding that the path to long-term success in the sales industry was not just a destination but rather a lifelong commitment to excellence and growth that transcended the boundaries of traditional business practices and positioned them as champions of sustainable success and innovation within the dynamic and ever-evolving landscape of the sales industry.

SUMMARY:

Sales Success: "Mastering the Art of Perpetual Sales"
" is a captivating narrative that chronicles the remarkable journey of Alex Mason, a seasoned sales professional whose unwavering dedication and innovative approach catapult him to the pinnacle of success in the competitive world of sales. From the initial struggles of navigating the cutthroat sales industry to the eventual triumphs of building enduring relationships and achieving unprecedented growth, Alex's story serves as a beacon of inspiration and guidance for aspiring sales professionals seeking to carve their own path to success.Throughout the novel, readers are immersed in the intricacies of the sales industry, delving into the nuances of customer engagement, effective communication, and the psychology of selling. Alex's strategic insights and practical wisdom offer readers a

comprehensive understanding of the art of salesmanship, emphasizing the importance of empathy, authenticity, and adaptability in fostering meaningful connections and driving sustainable growth within any organization.As the narrative unfolds, readers are taken on a transformative journey that explores the challenges and opportunities inherent in the ever-evolving sales landscape. Alex's resilience in the face of economic uncertainties and market fluctuations serves as a testament to the power of strategic planning, market analysis, and the cultivation of a resilient mindset in navigating through turbulent times and emerging stronger than before.Moreover, the novel highlights the transformative potential of embracing technology and innovation in driving sales excellence, emphasizing the significance of leveraging digital platforms, omni-channel marketing, and strategic partnerships to expand market reach and amplify brand presence. Alex's pioneering spirit and forward-thinking approach position him as a trailblazer in the realm of sales innovation, inspiring readers to embrace a culture of continuous learning, personal growth, and adaptability in their own pursuit of success within the dynamic and competitive landscape of the sales industry.Ultimately, "Sales Mastery: The Journey to Success" is more than just a narrative; it is a comprehensive guide that offers readers invaluable insights and practical strategies for achieving enduring success and fulfillment in the ever-evolving world of sales. Through Alex's story, readers are encouraged to embrace the transformative power of dedication, resilience, and innovation, and to embark on their own journey towards sales excellence and long-term success, armed with the wisdom and expertise shared within the pages of this compelling and insightful narrative.